A Perfect Circle of Sun

A Perfect
Circle of Sun

Linda Pastan

THE **SWALLOW PRESS** INC.

CHICAGO

Published by

The Swallow Press Incorporated
1139 South Wabash Avenue
Chicago, Illinois 60605

ISBN 0-8040-0553-2
LIBRARY OF CONGRESS CATALOG CARD NO. 76-171879

New Poetry Series Volume No. 44

This book is printed on 100% recycled paper.

Some of these poems have appeared in the
following periodicals:

The Chicago Tribune, Dryad, Epos,
The Literary Review, The Massachusetts Review,
The Michigan Quarterly, Midstream, Motive, The Nation,
The New York Times, Poet and Critic, Prickly Pear,
Quarterly Review of Literature, Poetry Northwest,
The Radcliffe Quarterly, The Sewanee Review, Sumac,
Shenendoah, Trace, Red Clay Reader, The University Review,
Voyages, The Washingtonian

To Ira

CONTENTS

1. JANUARY, 7 A.M.

Second Son

The lion and the lamb lie down together
in my son, blink at me from the pit
of his eyes, just as he draws the cover
down their cage for sleep. And sleepless I bear
the mildness of a child stripped of everything
in winter who blunders into a storm
of flakes seeing in them his lost fleece;
and the paw, tawny and sheathed as a cub's,
from which are loosed five switchblades of claw.

Arcadia

There is always a bare house,
one cumulous tree balanced
at the rim of the second story,
emblematic fields the color of change.
We almost find it beyond
the drawn shade of the bus,
beyond the drawn eyelid where light flickers westward,
at the far end of the train whistle
as we travel with George Willard,
with Nick Carroway, travel
towards Christmas and a house
wrapped as safely in scenery
as the corn in its layers of husk.
Birds fly past the chimney,
grow smaller,
disappear as the house disappears around
the flung arm of the road—
solid as a dream at the moment of waking.

Writing While My Father Dies

There is not a poem in sight,
only my father running out
upstairs, and me without a nickel
for the meter. The children hide
before the television
shivering in its glacial light,
and shivering I rub these words
together, hoping for a spark.

After X-ray

The bones are all there waiting their hour,
patient as hangers, pushed to the back of a closet,
on which this flesh is hung just for a while.
I feel them come to the surface slowly,
rise like their image in the developer's tank,
waiting to break through skin. And what can death
do with these bones? Planted like dry pods
in the earth they bloom later, washed clear of blood
to shine somewhere like strung beads of coral.

January, 7 A.M.

Albino morning.
Windows like milk glass.
Pale sun, pink-eyed;
paler moon frozen
fast to the flagpole's
tip, like the boy's tongue
in the old winter
story.

      Cold travels
the shallow nerve bed
with intimations
of toothache coming,
coming. Early cars
trail their exhausts thick
as the icy breath
of the milkman's horse,
long ago pastured.

At The Gynecologist's

The body so carefully
contrived for pain,
wakens from the dream of health
again and again
to hands impersonal as wax
and instruments that pry
into the closed chapters of flesh.
See me here, my naked legs
caught in these metal stirrups,
galloping towards death
with flowers of ether in my hair.

Distances

You travel across the room.
Two chairs and a table
are between us; the shapes
of your words are between us.
Straight and cold as railroad track
I lie in my old roadbed
measuring distances—
waiting for you to pass
over me once again,
on your way somewhere else.

Notes From The Delivery Room

Strapped down,
victim in an old comic book,
I have been here before,
this place where pain winces
off the walls
like too bright light.
Bear down a doctor says,
foreman to sweating laborer,
but this work, this forcing
of one life from another
is something that I signed for
at a moment when I would have signed anything.
Babies should grow in fields;
common as beets or turnips
they should be picked and held
root end up, soil spilling
from between their toes—
and how much easier it would be later,
returning them to earth.
Bear up . . . bear down . . . the audience
grows restive, and I'm a new magician
who can't produce the rabbit
from my swollen hat.
She's crowning, someone says,
but there is no one royal here,
just me, quite barefoot,
greeting my barefoot child.

Dirge

*"The extent of injury which can be directly attributed to occupa-
tion reached astounding proportions in the U.S. . . . ."*
INDUSTRIAL HYGIENE, BY WILSON SMILLIE

The poets are falling, falling
like leaves on a wind of their own words:
Dylan Thomas over the sheer edge of America;
Sylvia Plath (witch and Gretel combined)
into the hospitable oven.

The poets are plugging the dike with words,
then walking calmly into the sea.
Hart Crane on a Wednesday in slippery April,
Randall Jarrell, Delmore Schwartz, Weldon Kees.
And at the factory

girls paint time's face with radium
and slowly burn; miners slip, hand over hand,
into the blind grave.
Only poets safe at their desks hear death years away,
and full of the intensity of words,
rush to meet it.

Evening On The B. & O.

I have a fool's face,
transparent as a ghost's
on the train window;
the dusk unravels
behind it in lengths
of telegraph wire
as I stare with fool's
eyes at trees, their green
light just going out.

Rainy Season

The temperature of discontent
is 104 in the steaming shade
of my tongue or high up
under the armpit where the red
mercury in the thermometer
is the only color left
in all the world.

This is my rainy season;
its tears are sweet but unquenching
like soda pop the children drink
until they gag on it.
The mocking bird has come
for the red holly berries;

she swallows them whole,
chases away the cardinal
and the jay and mocks my sad voice
as the squirrels mock me
with their insolent tails,
high in the bird feeder.

Grey, grey, the world shivers
under dust covers of stale snow
and I have caught its chill.
Come shake down the thermometer with care
or the glass will go flying,
and I will break out of my skin
in a thousand dangerous fragments.

2. EARLY WALK

Skylight

I sit in a perfect circle of sun
in a room without windows
where pale walls grow stencilled flowers
and see the tops of real trees,
see real leaves flickering in the light
as the tongues of garter snakes flicker
or flattening under an east wind
as if they grew in rushing water.
I think of a ruined church in Rome
where a boy in a blue shirt threw sticks
at a wall that had disappeared
who knows when,
or of something I only read of,
a man whose stomach was a window
doctors gazed through at organs
opening for food like tropic plants
beneath the floor of a glass bottomed boat.
And here in the center of this house
deep under shingles, under tar paper,
under plaster pale as unsunned flesh
I see through one round skylight the real world
held up to the sun by its heels and moving—
it is like candling eggs.

To My Son, Approaching 11

I outgrew childhood once,
served the full sentence
of innocence myself,
grew scales and callouses
to cover all but the
under parts of memory,
a rotting tree trunk
with green vines growing
through its old knot holes
like flowers through the
sockets of a skull.
Stephen, in more than sleep
recurrent dreams come true:
I live it all awake with you.

Early Walk

Now it is April,
not even sleeping bears are safe—
their hollow logs pinch them awake
like outgrown shoes.
We take an early walk and stop to kiss.
Beyond my head you face the woods
where green has caught like a slow fire
and starts to spread.
I see beyond your head
two roses clenched like fists
against the kitchen wall
and think of tea brewing to bitterness
in its forgotten pot. And still we kiss
and close our eyes against such separateness—
not even sleeping bears are safe.

At Bingham Falls, Vermont

There were no waterfalls in Eden,
no pure curves of force streaming downhill
like wet stallions eager to mate with rock.
There were no brambles, no raspberries.
The fruit was smooth as wax and fit the palm,
and only the curve of the giraffe's neck
bending to drink made ripples in those still ponds.
Later when the garden gate had rusted
off its hinge the pears turned brown, and honeysuckle
subtle as the snake crept around trees.
In all the honky tonk of second growth
did water too go wild! And what child of Cain
hearing that roar even in his sleep
thought to enslave it, to chain it to a wheel
for grinding his winter wheat to flour?

Elevation 700 Feet

The fireflies go on and off
as soundlessly as harbor lights—
or are those harbor lights? The sun
has gone back to the sea, taking
with it the color from the trees
and every other natural
boundary. Here on this overlook
I am in time for the last view.
Just for a little while valley
and ocean roll at my feet
as casually as bolts of cloth
dropped on the tailor's workroom floor.
The seabirds darkening to bats
shake the water from their wings,
and waves go back and forth in
endless parody of parting.
Better for me the long descent,
carsick and weary behind
a slow bus, and the view only
a flick of moonlight caught in the
car's fender at every curve.

April (2)

Spring comes in bursts—
new leaves teething
down the bare length
of a branch, sun
dusty as pollen
on the drawn shade,
neon forsythia.
The nuthatch squeezes
its fat family
into the wren house,
ferns uncurl like
long stemmed snails, and
in the next street
rain barely falls,
leaving its pale
watercolor wash.

April (3)

The young cherry trees
stick out their limbs
as awkwardly as foals
standing for the first time.
Around them the maples
are itchy with new growth,
and dogwoods stand
in ballet poses.
How many leaves
open their green shutters now
to let April through.

At The Jewish Museum

("The Lower East Side: Portal To American Life, 1887-1924")

We can endure the eyes
of these children lightly,
because they stare
from the faces of our fathers
who have grown old before us.
Their hungers have always been
our surfeit. We turn again
from the rank streets, from
marred expectancies and laundry
that hangs like a portent
over everything.
Here in a new museum
we walk past all the faces
the cameras have stolen from time.
We carry them like piecework
to finish at home,
knowing how our childrens' sins
still fall upon the old Jew
in a coal cellar, on Ludlow street,
in Nineteen hundred.

View

A boy, somebody else's child, dribbles
his basketball around my greenest tree.
How do I tell him that he mars my view,
sends his ripples through my window glass
as surely as a stone dropping its implications
in circles of water? The tree he uses
I call mine, keeping it for the signals
its leaves send up like flags: vigilance;
solemnity; to bear whatever
the season inflicts—the encroaching moss,
months of abrasive ice, the cramps of thaw
after January's deep anaesthetic.
I have watched it concentrate on its own roots,
have seen how pitilessly it hoards the light
when there is not enough to go around.
And now this boy comes, blending his shade
quite carelessly with the tree's, laughing
until each syllable of leaf laughs back,
throwing his basketball straight at the sun.

Adam Remembering

We lived in such sweet chaos, once.
The cats slept on the Sunday Times,
flies buzzed, lost in a maze of sugar,
a bird pecked at the tassels of a lamp.
Nothing was named yet, nothing numbered.
We loved each other as we pleased,
on the blue bathroom tiles, like fish
or in the dusty flower beds,
absolved by heat.
For middle age we kept one yellow cat,
the smell of apples rotting in a bowl,
the surprise of endings.

Emily Dickinson

We think of her hidden in a white dress
among the folded linens and sachets
of well kept cupboards, or just out of sight
sending jellies and notes with no address
to all the wondering Amherst neighbors.
Eccentric as New England weather
the stiff wind of her mind, stinging or gentle,
blew two half imagined lovers off.
Yet legend won't explain the sheer sanity
of vision, the serious mischief
of language, the economy of pain.

Passover

I

I set my table with metaphor:
the curling parsely—green sign nailed to the doors
of God's underground; salt of desert and eyes;
the roasted shank bone of a Pascal lamb,
relic of sacrifice and bleating spring.
Down the long table, past fresh shoots of a root
they have been hacking at for centuries,
you hold up the unleavened bread—a baked scroll
whose wavy lines are undecipherable.

II

The wise son and the wicked, the simple son
and the son who doesn't ask, are all my son
leaning tonight as it is written,
slouching his father calls it. His hair is long;
hippie hair, hassid hair, how strangely alike
they seem tonight.
　　　　　First Born, a live child cried
among the bullrushes, but the only root
you know stirs between your legs, ready
to spill its seed in gentile gardens.
And if the flowers be delicate and fair,
I only mind this one night of the year
when far beyond the lights of Jersey,
Jerusalem still beckons us, in tongues.

III

What black throated bird
in a warm country
sings spirituals,
sings spirituals
to Moses now?

IV

One exodus prefigures the next.
The glaciers fled before hot whips of air.
Waves bowed at God's gesture
for fugitive Israel to pass;
while fish, caught then behind windows
of water, remembered how their brothers once
pulled themselves painfully from the sea,
willing legs to grow
from slanted fins.
Now the blossoms pass from April's tree,
refugee raindrops mar the glass,
borders are transitory.
And the changeling gene, still seeking
stone sanctuary, moves on.

V

Far from Egypt, I have sighted blood,
have heard the throaty mating of frogs.
My city knows vermin, animals loose in hallways,
boils, sickness, hail.
In the suburban gardens
seventeen year locusts rise
from their heavy beds
in small explosions of sod.
Darkness of newsprint.
My son, my son.

3. *SUMMER IS ONLY CAMOUFLAGE*

At Woods Hole

site of the Marine Biological Laboratory

To measure the straight line of a mast,
the angle of wave, dune, spread sail
is all the geometry of this shore—
and the shark's fin on its way to kill
bisecting the arc of a half-moon
on its way to sea.

A sunfish tacking into the wind
or the gull dropping a locked clam
on ledges of rock below
is the psychology of this shore;
and the edge of the sea unravelling
from here to Hatteras
all of its history.

And we learn nothing, lying
on sand hot and pliant as each other's flesh,
making our promises while rows of cars gleam
in the distance like beached mackerel,
and waves seem to bring the water in forever
even as the tide moves surely out.

The Last Train

*"The long-distance passenger train has moved one step nearer to
extinction: on July 26 The New York Central said it intends to
discontinue all trains running over 200 miles . . . ."*

U.S. NEWS & WORLD REPORT

There may have been a boy,
lying in a cabin in the subtle place
where field and plain each goes its separate way,
who fell asleep to the muffled drumming of buffalo
as, dark and shaggy as sleep itself,
they traveled past his window towards extinction.

Now in a house at the edge of the same plain,
another boy lets consciousness recede
on the receding whistle of a train
passing his open window for the last time,
leaving behind a spike or rusted nails
like arrowheads or pieces of dried bone.

So we are left,
each boy, each sleeper,
to the single, abstract tone of the jet plane.
We follow sleep as well as we are able
along disintegrating paths of vapor,
high above the dreamlike shapes of clouds.

Penelope

The sun is scarcely
a shadow of itself,
it bled into the sea
all last week
and now, bandaged away,
waits out with me the long, long
month of rain.

Grey fades to grey.
The horizon is
the finest seam between
water and water, sky and sky.
Only the tide still moves,
leaving the print of its ribbed bones
on the abandoned sand
as you left yours on me
when you moved imperceptibly from my embrace.

I must wring out the towels,
wring out the swim suits,
wring my eyes dry of tears,
watching at a window
on one leg, then the other,
like the almost extinct heron.

To A Second Son

Now you embrace chameleons
changing color yourself with the scenery,
white with me and my white questions,
muted under a sky bruised
black and blue.

You feed your lizards
moths, plundered each evening
from the porch light
while my shudder records
as accurately as a seismograph
the distance between us.

Peter, we have given you
these hand me downs:
your brother's half used sweater,
your father's reel,
and all my old faults
drowned once like a bagful of cats.

They have washed up twenty years downstream
bloated and mewing, to plague
the perfect body you will grow into,
shaking all of us delicately off.

Wood

My daughter at almost three
rehearses for her life all day
with acquiescent dolls and blocks
that form strange alphabets
of prophecy. I watch,
fearing the evil eye
of milkmen and housecats,
the bland malevolence of stairs,
the viruses that come
even through the mailslot,
so hungry are they for cells.
Beauty ignites its own slow fuse.
Helpless I knock and knock on wood,
on cribslats, on pencils,
on the bottoms of chairs,
and now on this rough tree trunk
I drag into the house
and shamefaced christen roofbeam.

Camouflage

Diffused with the color
of the stone it rests on,
the chameleon turns from simile
to metaphor and back to lizard.
Summer is only camouflage.
Under the thick disguise of leaves
wait last winter's old trees;
the earth is raw clay
under a cowl of topsoil.
And what of us, walking
the spindly boardwalk,
smiles chainlinked across bone?
We say the waves like rosaries,
hour on hour, and later
flat against the sand
turn beach colored ourselves.

Beech Avenue: The Fourth Of July

How heavy the summer seems, how thick-waisted
and full of heat. The elm is swollen with leaves,
and the lowing clouds, still filled with rain,
hang pendulous as unmilked udders.
The air tastes faintly of cordite where
a Roman candle flickers and is snuffed out.
One by one the minutes gather and spill
over the rim of my cupped hands, and I
watch as though already remembering
these friends scattered like spit watermelon seeds
over the garden; Rachel holding
her first amazing sparkler; the boys
running through grass away from us, from
the whole green day which nonetheless will keep
hard as a pebble around which moss will grow
and lichen. Where shall I be on that July
when the pebble cracks like a geode,
and there perfectly preserved in layers
of crystal my grown sons find these very
trees, short-circuited with fireflies,
this restless lightning, locked in cloud but
hammering out now, sparks flying, as rain
hesitant all day finally starts to fall?

Plaint

There is a figure in every landscape—
a boy at the other end of the pier,
a woman picking dandelions for salad
who leaves a kneeprint hidden in the grass
like the watermark on whitest paper.
That crooked branch is really a girl's arm
sunned to the very color of the bark,
an oval leaf conceals an oval eye:
children are climbing here, or have been.
Even in Adam's garden in the green
newness of unused shade, distrusting
privacy, God placed a sleeping woman.

Libation, 1966

We used to sacrifice young girls,
killing them like does
on rocky altars
they themselves had kept
tidy as kitchens.

Moloch took babies,
picked them early
from their mother's limbs
like green fruit,
spat out the pits.

It always was for some necessity,
fat harvest,
rain,
wind for a flaccid ocean, sails
flapping like a gull's wings towards Troy.

Now we give young men.
They dance as delicately
as any bull boy,
with bayonette,
in a green maze,
under a sky as hot as Crete.

Evening At Bird Island

I travel to bird island
with only oars for wings,
dragging a wake
like an outstretched gull
through colors
the moon will salt to grey.

Unfastened
the birds rise and rise,
and I, searching for crane or heron,
find only wings
two pencil lines apiece—
a child's drawing of flight.

The gulls come in to sleep,
fold with a sound of feathers
like sheets rustling,
and I fold,
arms wrapped around knees
in the bottom of a boat
that seems to sink
in its own reflection.

In quiet water
under my rocking floor
fish swallow other fish,
feeding
like bad dreams
under the surfaces of sleep.

On The Road To The Harbor Tunnel

A boneyard of old cars
rusts away in all
the positions of love.
The sun rusts away
in the evasive west.
There are auguries to read
in these mechanical
entrails of Baltimore
before we also learn
the taste of metal.

I Waken Under Eaves

I waken under eaves
to light slanting up towards morning
and curtains filling like sails
ready to come about in a slow wind.
I fell asleep to the longing of crickets.
They rubbed their legs together
through a foliage of dreams,
changing now to small, nervous birds
that search the splintered windowsills
for crumbs. Beyond waits the sea
ready to pour its salt in all my wounds,
reminding me that you have gone,
that summer is going.
I roll between safe sheets
away from windows, from this morning
which like the others will break
its promises of light.
My own horizon is sure; it is the place
where the sloped ceiling meets the floor
in this my one, my final attic.

Williamsburg

"History, Stephen said, is a nightmare from which I am trying to awake."
JAMES JOYCE, ULYSSES

Unscrew the locks from the doors!
Unscrew the doors themselves from their jambs.
WALT WHITMAN, SONG OF MYSELF

I The Market Square

These houses in their muted brick seem
smaller than life, smaller surely than the dead
who stare us down from centerfolds of books.
The Washington of Valley Forge would
have to bend historic knees to fit
that trundle bed, and Patrick Henry,
slogans flying from his mouth like buckshot—
his fist in emphasis would split the delicate
gate legged tables. Only the sky feels adequate,
a million flecks of southern dust settling into
a distant, pilgrim blue, elusive as history.

II The Visitors Center

And we are
tourists still,
gazing with
something like
anguish in—
to the rooms
of other
lives, reaching
behind a
velvet rope
when no one
watches, to
touch something
authentic.

III The Craft Shops

The basketmaker, in knee breeches
and a leather apron,
sits by an 18th century fire weaving baskets
like old spells
to any shape or size.
I have watched him strip a sapling with his axe,
cut his reeds to measure,
pass the slim weft of memory deftly
through the warp of death.
Two hundred years have gone,
ground with the corn in the arms of the mill,
while a new generation of horses stamps and coughs
in the same old stalls.
So little time: the space
from Athens to Sparta or from Jamestown here.
I reach across this small abyss to touch
the basketmaker's hand,
but a Woolworth pencil falling from his pocket
spins like a wand,
and there rises between us a wall of baskets,
baskets of bolts and screws, of old hubcaps,
beercans, and the broken
filaments of lightbulbs
gone dark
before my father's father dreamed America.

IV The Colonial Gardens

With what musical strictness
the songbirds guard their own brief
territories, even here
where freedom is endemic.

V The Governor's Palace

I am waiting by the canal.
A few violets are scattered near the bench like footnotes,
everything else is perfectly green.
Now the cries of children rise from the formal maze,
and the cameras whir and click, persistent
as locusts in the wavy air.
In the governor's palace
the tourists browze like responsible cattle
under a portrait of the governor's wife.
Her face is formal and still.
Around her, slaves lose themselves
in the darkening canvas;
only their eyes show up and their white caps,
like the ghosts of moths who will haunt our screens forever.
Children, come out of the labyrinth,
though the minotaur bears your mother's name
and your father's horns. You will trip on the fine grass,
cut your delicate hands on the clipped hedges.
Play instead in the kitchen garden.
Discover the bright yams
pulled from the earth, round and bursting as udders,
the black soil still clinging to their roots
like water.
Search out the young peas, already impatient
in their pods.
Learn the new, green taste of raw beans.

4. OCTOBER FUNERAL

After Reading Nelly Sachs

Poetry has opened all my pores,
and pain as colorless as gas
moves in. I notice now the bones
that weld my child together
under her fragile skin; the crowds
of unassuming leaves that wait
on every corner for burning;
even your careless smile—bright teeth
that surely time will cut through
like a rough knife kerneling corn.

September

In windy fall
the landscape flaps like laundry
hung between two trees,
and expectations fly around my head,
blow out of reach
like all these leaves.
The habit of beginning
is hard to break.
I grow nostalgic
for someone else's childhood,
watching a sky
as clear as unlined paper
for old secrets scribbled in the margins.
Wait.
The school doors close behind the children
shutting some fact inside,
some special decimal
or the names of kings.
Is that what I watch for
here by the door?
Winter is expected, nothing more,
and yet things seemed transfused
with new blood—
turning the woods red.

Each Autumn

Each autumn seasons us for death.
We put our leaves in order,
raking, burning, acknowledging
the persistence of time.
We have been dying all our lives,
waiting out the slow seasons
of the blood,
tramping the leaves to dust
under our own forgetting feet.
Only the trees go down in light,
welcoming winter. Listen
to the first snow fall from the ruined branch
with the same sound as earth
thrown into a new grave.

Between Generations

I left my father in a wicker basket
on other people's doorsteps.
Now I wait to be adopted by children,
wait in a house far between generations
with night rising faster
than the moon.

I dream of Regan laughing on her father's lap
behind the castle.
I laughed once in my father's face,
and he laughed, and the two laughters
locked like bumpers
that still rust away between us.

My children fill the house with departures.
Zippers close, trunks close, wire hangers jump
on the empty pole—ghosts without their sheets.
And I ask what strict gravity
pushes love down the steep incline
from father to child, always down?

Morning

Aeneas

Such strangers as we were
lay tangled among sheets,
building our dreams from the same
oxygen. I am no tide
to be the moon's slave.
Holding my anguish close as sleep
I put a wall of smoke between us
with the day's first cigarette.

Dido

We fall into pretended sleep
and waken to the aftertaste
of aged dreams.
Gravity is against us, pulling
our bodies apart;
September is against us,
pulling down summer leaf by leaf.
Stay with me a little longer,
listen to the ticking
of my overwound heart
as it runs down to silence.

Yom Kippur

A tree beside the synagogue atones
of all its leaves. Within the ram's horn blows
and sins come tumbling down to rest among
old cigarettes and handkerchiefs. My sins
are dried and brittle now as any leaves
and barely keep me warm. I have atoned
for them before, burned clean by October,
lulled by the song of a fasting belly.
But sins come creeping back like unwed girls,
and leaves return to willing trees for spring.

Prognosis

The electric clock swallows
its own ticking, the seconds
multiply silently, like cells.
We are infected with time,
show the rash already.
This actuality
catches me in a swinging door
leaving me dizzy and breathless
on the harsh pavement. And yet
the girl across the street
is sweeping leaves calmly,
a man waits at the bus stop
putting off death to run
some other errand. If they saw me
would they catch fear like an attack
of yawning? Would they beat and scratch
leaving the water muddy
over our heads? But people
die politely nowadays;
even as the plane tenses
to hit the mountain, a hostess
pours out coffee, and passengers
keep staring at the moon,
starched and impersonal
as a nurse's cap.

October Funeral: For Ag

The world is shedding
its thousand skins.
The snake goes naked,
and the needles of the pine fall out
like the teeth of a comb I broke
upon your hair last week.
The ghosts of dead leaves
haunt no one. Impossible
to give you to the weather,
to leave you locked in a killed tree.
No metaphysic has prepared us
for the simple act of turning
and walking away.

Journey's End

How hard we try to reach death safely,
luggage intact, each child accounted for,
the wounds of passage quickly bandaged up.
We treat the years like stops along the way
of a long flight from the catastrophe
we move to, thinking: home free all at last.
Wave, wave your hanky towards journey's end;
avert your eyes from windows grimed with twilight
where landscapes rush by, terrible and lovely.

A Dangerous Time

November is a dangerous time for trees;
November is a dangerous time.
The leaves darken,
the sun goes on and off
beyond strange clouds,
a wolf is at the door.
Upstairs the children toss through dreams,
hearing the wind in the keyholes of sleep,
hearing the sirens circle the house like coyotes.
I have tucked them in with the wolf's own story,
how it grew from a cub, devoured the bride,
blew down the house of straw—
how this was natural.
Now my eldest walks the freezing hills
crying wolf, wolf.
He is a prophet, he has warned before
that the stars will rise like gooseflesh,
and a wolf is at the door.